Max Zaps Spots

by Vikram Russo
illustrated by Audrey Durney

Practice Decodable 10

McGraw Hill Education

Bothell, WA • Chicago, IL • Columbus, OH • New York, NY

MHEonline.com

Send all inquiries to:
McGraw-Hill Education
8787 Orion Place
Columbus, OH 43240

ISBN: 978-0-02-143437-4
MHID: 0-02-143437-9

Printed in the United States of America.

8 9 10 CTM 23

At his job, Max has rags.

See all the spots on his rags?

See all the spots on Max?

Suds zip up and zap spots!

Not a spot is on the rags.

Not a spot is on Max!